DAYS IN DEVONPORT
Part 7

Gerald W. Barker

Dedicated to the Freedom of the Plymouth Toll Gates, Tuesday, April 1st, 1924.

In Loving Memory
OF THE
HALF-PENNY GATE
whose career was finished by the
Mayor & Corporation in State.

After the years I've bled you
 Of half-pennies to pass my way,
Its no wonder you are all smiling
 Over my demise to-day.
I've took toll of your Grandfather's
  Grandfather,
Your Grandmother's Grandmother too,
And also their great great grandparents
 As well as taking it from you.
I'd have taken it from your children's
  children,
 And also their children as well
If I had only been allowed to go on
 Instead of being consigned to—finis.
Composed by " Red."

Now we pay no longer,
 From to-day its free,
No more will you pay for the pleasure
 Of walking over me.
I should have been " done in "
 Five score years ago,
For a town the size of Plymouth
 My finish has been very slow.

For Devonport youngsters who could not afford the half-penny to cross the bridge from Devonport to Stonehouse, there was no easy solution at high tide as the water reached as far as the Military Hospital at Millbridge. 1st April, 1924 was, therefore, a day of celebration when the Toll Gates "Career" was finished by the Mayor and Corporation.

This version of the book is virtually as originally published, presenting the work of Gerald W Barker. There are now additional pages at the back providing information about the publisher, Arthur L Clamp.

The republishing project is being managed by Arthur's grandson, Steven Gibson. We aim to find all the research that he was involved in publishing, preserving it for the next generation as part of 'The Clamp Collection'.

INTRODUCTION

By letter and by word of mouth I am indebted to all those people that have given me so much information about Devonport. These are some of the contributions by some of the people:-

Mrs. Bryant, who was born in 1899, remembers when 8 years old attending the school at Keppel Place that was eventually knocked down to make way for the erection of the Higher Educational School later to become Stoke Damerel High School for Girls. Her mother and father ran horse buses in Kingsand and Cawsand. After catching the funnel ferry from Cremyll to the King Billy Statue she remembers having a choice of five ways to get to the school, viz. (i) by way of the Devonport monument, (ii) along Richmond Walk, (iii) up over Mount Wise slopes and passing by the Captain Scott memorial, (iv) through Fore Street or (v) via the Southern Station and crossing over the railway bridge that was forbidden territory to the pupils.

"I was with Bugler William Lake (World renowned Devonport boxer) when he was killed by bombs that fell on the Dockyard in 1941." Mr. Wall lived at one time in Canterbury Street in Devonport.

"I was born in Stoke in 1899 and lived there until I was grown up..... My father was the owner of Swiss's in Marlborough Street. In my young days the Alhambra was called the Metropole, but I was never allowed to go there!" *Dora Rolston née Swiss.*

Albert Henry Hadley played a banjolin to the car queues at Torpoint Ferry between the wars. As a young man he was wounded when a soldier in the Dardanelles in World War I. The bullet had to remain with him the rest of his life. However it didn't prevent him earning enough as a 'busker' to bring up a family of six girls and two boys. *John Alexander Hadley, son.*

I can identify one member of the camp photograph on page 12 (part I) entitled "Some Devonport Men". In the centre row second from the left is my father Albert Hurden who lived in Drummond Place off Albert Road. He was born in 1891. He was about 18 years old in the photo. My only suggestion as to the possible occasion is a Rugger match (15 people!) on St. David's Day — they seem to be wearing daffodils in their buttonholes. *Mrs. Joan Gilmore, daughter.*

My father Frederick Niles who was born in St. Aubyn Street was in the Navy and so was my grandfather William Niles and my great grandfather also called William Niles. My great great grandfather was also in the Navy. *Mrs. Joan Bice.*

Acknowledgements

My thanks to the following for their help in making the publication of this book possible. Mrs. C. Gardner, Mrs. J. Fitzpatrick, Mrs. J. R. Gribell, Mr. L. E. Meech-Noyes, Mr. R. Smith, Mr. R. Rundell, Secretary of the Hertfordshire Postcard Club, Mrs. V. Anstis, Miss M. Gordon, Mrs. B. Elliot, Mrs. W. Rogers, Mrs. I. Daley, Mr. H. Feabes, Mr. S. P. Greenwood, Mr. H. H. Greenwood, Mrs. E. A. Bryant, Mr. G. Fleming, Mrs. L. M. Hooper, Mr. P. F. Ghillyer, Mrs. W. Bartlett, Mr. S. Warwick, Mrs. M. Bonning, Mr. P. A. Lancaster, Mr. F. E. Pine, Administrator of Devonport Hospital, Mr. L. Presland, X-Ray Department of Derriford Hospital. The meaning of the initials *G.W.R.* in its 150th Anniversary is well known nationally. Locally well known are the initials *A.L.C.* These could well stand for "A Lively Contributor" as far as his work on our environmental history is concerned. My thanks once again to Arthur L. Clamp for his help in compiling *Days in Devonport* part 7.

Gerald W. Barker,
44 Burnham Park Road,
Peverell,
Plymouth PL3 5QD

Who's for Tennis?

This later became, "Who's for an operation?" when the tennis court at the rear of the Royal Albert Hospital became the extended operating theatre in the latter years of its life. The original operating theatre was able to have north light through its roof which was helpful during operations. The bridge was a covered way that led from the hospital exit to the nurses home. To the left of the covered way (looking at the photo) were Charles Lander ward and Mayhew ward, The Emma ward and Staff dining room. The Harry Wright and Washbourn wards were also to the left, out of sight. The staff quarters and side ward were to the right of the covered way.

The Room With a View

Devonport Park could be seen from the kitchen window when this photograph was taken one year before the hospital closed in 1983. In the 1920's the kitchens were to the left of the operating theatre (facing) and above them was the board-room and the Matron's sitting room. The tower to the right (in the above photo) is one of two still remaining. The top ward in the tower was the Adams ward and the lower one the Norman ward with the x-ray department below it. Here, too, were the sanitary annexes, w.c. and sluices.

Ward Decorations

Inside the ward the polished floor and pictures on the walls add lustre to the decorations. Sometimes a dance would be held in the Royal Albert Hospital (Extension Ward) later to be named Charles Lander. Tickets sold, in aid of the Plymouth Voluntary Hospital funds, were five shillings and sixpence (27½p) which included supper! A Bridge Room was available for non-dancers. Music on Friday, 17th May 1929 was provided by Mr. Albert Fullbrook and his band from 9 p.m. to 2 a.m.

The Brown Bear

What is a Brown Bear doing amidst all the demolition of the Devonport Hospital in 1983? It is in fact the public house of that name in Chapel Street depicted on the mural in the lower right hand corner. The Housemen were responsible for the painting which also shows the Torpoint Ferry approaching the hospital. The mural was on the wall of the doctors' common room. In the 1920s this was known as the Board room.

Royal Albert Hospital, Devonport

Devonport's Derry's Clock

As Derry's Clock was to Plymouth so the lamp post in the centre of the road near the hospital (cover of Part 5) was to Devonport people. "See you by the horse trough" wouldn't have sounded so romantic to young men like the Royal Marines standing outside the main gate in 1906. The ornate lamp post was still well remembered by members of a group to whom the author spoke about "Days in Devonport" in 1985. They believed the lamp post was erased in the late 1920s.

They Also Serve

The Carnival Queen and attendants are in the grounds of Devonport Hospital. Others, too, did much to help their fellow citizens. Those who organised the 30 or so pigeons that flew blood and other specimens between the hospital and the loft at Freedom Fields Hospital made the Devonport Hospital world famous for this particular service. The pigeon service was introduced in 1979 to save money on taxis carrying specimens between hospitals. With the closing of Devonport Hospital in 1983 most of the pigeons were returned to their original owners.

Great Expectations

The people of Devonport make ready to welcome H.R.H. the Prince of Wales in 1904. Fore Street was the scene of many processions. On the 4th July 1814 the Dockyard mechanics with their officers commemorated the establishment of peace with each branch being led by the emblems of the respective trades in the shape of models. On 8th September 1831 a similar procession through Fore Street took place in honour of the Coronation of King William IV and his Royal Consort Queen Adelaide.

Devonport's Queen

"Queen Devonia" and her Court are greeted by enthusiastic subjects. The magnificent Guildhall in Devonport was a setting fit for the Queen, as she made her way via Ker Street for the coronation in Devonport Park about 1929.

G.W.R.

The summer of 1985 marks the celebrations of the 150th anniversary of the Great Western Railway. The initials G.W.R. on the carriages to many enthusiasts stood for, *God's Wonderful Railway*. A train similar to the one in the photograph, painted in G.W.R. cream and chocolate livery was at the Friary depot in July, 1985. Crowds watched as Jimmy Young put out his programme as part of the Radio Two Railshow, to celebrate the 150 years. The special exhibition train visited over 40 locations that used to be served by the G.W.R.

ROYAL NAVAL BARRACKS BOYS' BRIGADE.

Standing Orders

(Revised May, 1940)

Devonport:
Royal Naval Barracks Printing Office,
May, 1940.

Formation and Object.

The Brigade was formed in November, 1906, for the sons of Commissioned Warrant. Officers, Warrant Officers, and Active Service Naval Ratings, with the following objects:—

1. Improvement of physique.
2. Inculcating habits of Punctuality, Cleanliness, and Obedience.
3. To teach Gunnery, Drill, Shooting, Seamanship, Swimming, Life Saving, First Aid, Armourers' Work, and Signals; Games, Dancing, Physical Training.

Organisation.

Officers, &c.—President, The Commodore, R.N. Barracks, Commanding Officer, Officer Instructor, 3 Gunners' Mates, 1 Chief Ordnance Artificer, 1 Physical Training Instructor, 1 Sick Berth Steward.

Uniform

One of the Standing Orders states:- Uniform is the property of the Brigade and consists of serge jumper and trousers, black silk handkerchief, blue jean collar, jersey, cap and ribbon, flannel dickey, and gaiters. As uniform is provided free duration of membership must be a minimum of 2 years. Black boots must be worn with uniform. One of the trophies competed for annually was the Morice Town Cup presented for attendance.

Young Sailor

Lionel Ernest Meech-Noyes is standing at ease outside the front door of 4 Milne Place. The author's young brother was a member of the R.N.B.B.B. (Royal Naval Barrack Boys Brigade). The age of enrolment was 10. On leaving school, like many other Devonport boys, he joined the Merchant Navy, and is now serving as a Chief Engineer.

Combined Bands 1930s

The Royal Naval and Royal Marine Bands are ready to play on the parade ground of the Royal Naval Barracks. In the background, one of the large capital ships of the Royal Navy lies at anchor. On Thursday March 28th 1985 the Combined Bands of Her Majesty's Royal Marines (Commando Forces and Training Forces) performed for the last time in public under their present names.

Oops! Sorry

This photograph is probably the last one taken of Devonport Park's tennis pavilion. It was taken by the author a few days before being knocked down due to a Plymouth City Council blunder in 1984. The officials said that it was an administrative error which misinterpreted a decisions list before the final demolition go-ahead was given. The survivor of many bombs that fell in the park during the Second World War, the pavilion held a lot of memories for many people.

Subscriptions Please

The R.F.C. (Royal Flying Corps) is commemorated on this memorial apart from the army and navy both being more closely associated with Devonport. It wasn't until 1st April, 1918 that the Royal Air Force came into existence, replacing the Royal Flying Corps and the Royal Naval Air Service. Mr. S. P. Greenwood remembers each pupil at his school being given a plan of the Devonport War Memorial in 1920 to take home to show parents for a subscription. *Any evening any day ..... you'll find them all doing the Lambeth Walk.* This was one of the many joyous dances that Devonport people joined in round the bandstand until the war started in 1939. The musical, *Me and My Girl,* is now being staged at the Adelphi Theatre in London.

BARRACKS			BARRACKS	
GEORGE			**LANE**	
"Musketry Arms"	56		Grocers Shop	57
Tenanted	55			58
GEORGE			"Half Moon" Inn	59
Butchers Shop	54		**STREET**	
Tenanted	53		"Kings Arms" Hotel	60
Viggers Dairy	52		Bakers Shop	61
ST STEPHEN			Plymouth Bretheren Mission Roo	
"Bristol Vaults" Inn	51		**STREET**	
Butchers Shop	50		General Shop	62
Marine Store Dealers	49		Sweet Shop	63
Tenanted	48		General Shop	64
Haberdashery Shop	47		Off License	65
General Shop	46		Tenanted	66
Tenanted	45		General Shop	67
Tenanted	44		Tenanted	68
Stephen's Dairy	43		Tenanted	69
Tenanted	42		Tenanted	70
Beer Retailer	41		Dairy	71
Tenanted	40		Hairdresser	72
Newsvendor	39		Tenanted	73
Beer Retailer	38		Butchers Shop	74
QUARRY			Bakery	75
"Himalaya" Inn	37		**STREET**	
General Shop	36		Greengrocers	76
Grocers Shop	35		Butchers Shop	77
Refreshment House	34		Grocer	78
Beer Retailer	33		General Shop	79
Bakery	32		Butchers Shop	80
China Shop	31		Tripe Shop	81
"Jolly Bacchus" Inn	30		Fish Shop	82
General Shop	29		Butchers Shop	83
"Royal Oak" Hotel	28		Bakery	84
FORT			Tenanted	85
General Shop	27		Tenanted	86
Boot Makers Shop	26		**STREET**	
General Shop	25		General Shop	87
Beer Retailer	24		Toy Shop	88
General Shop	23		Newsvendor	89
Chemist Shop	22		Tenanted	90
Tenanted	21		Pawnbroker	91
Grocers Shop	20		Tenanted	92
Hairdresser	19		Tenanted	93
"Albion Hotel"	18		Tobacconist Shop	94
CANTERBURY			Bakery	95
Bakery	17		"Rose & Crown" Hotel	96
"Royal Sovereign" Inn	16		**STREET**	
Greengrocers	15		General Shop	97
Fish Shop	14		General Shop	98
"George" Inn	13		**BAPTIST CHAPEL**	
Tenanted	12		Dairy	99
Bakery	11		General Shop	100
Tenanted	10		Tenanted	101
Haberdashery Shop	9		General Shop	102
MONUMENT			Mission Rooms	103
Beer Retailer	8		**STREET**	
Shoe Shop	7		General Shop	104
Beer Retailer	6		Grocer	105
Shinners Bakery	5		Tenanted	106
PIPE LANE			Lamp Oil Dealer	107
Tenanted	2		Bakery	108
"Royal Exchange" Hotel	1		Chemist / Post Office	109

JAMES STREET / PEMBROKE STREET

CENTRAL CHANCERY OF
THE ORDERS OF KNIGHTHOOD,
ST JAMES'S PALACE, S.W.1.

14th September 1976

Sir,

I am commanded to forward the Imperial Service Medal which Her Majesty The Queen has been graciously pleased to award to you in recognition of the meritorious services which you have rendered.

I have the honour to be, Sir,

Your obedient servant,

A.B. Curtis.

Registrar of the Imperial Service Order.

Stanley Philip Greenwood, Esq.

Meritorious Service

As an Engine Room Artificer serving in the Royal Navy the author has been one of many that have had reason to be glad of the efficiency "down below" due to the first class skills of the Dockyard workers. Stanley Philip Greenwood entered as an apprentice and later became an inspector. His brother, Horace H. Greenwood became a Foreman. The brothers are typical of those whose skills made Devonport Dockyard one of the finest in the world.

King's Hill

The building was erected in 1822 to recall the visit of H.M. King George III to the Dockyard. His Majesty admired the surrounding scenery. When "going ashore" the author remembers approaching the site by a winding path, passing a grotto and an ornamental fountain. Before leaving through the Mutton Cove Gates (first opened in 1891) in the proximity of the King Billy statue, one can see the beautiful slopes of Mount Edgcumbe.

Big Figurehead is Watching You

Small Devonport boys found figureheads, such as the one at the entrance to South Yard, awe inspiring. An even more frightening experience happened to a boy in 1741 when William Wallin was whipped at the gate for stealing two iron bolts valued at one shilling and sixpence. (7½p)

21st November, 1918

British sailors wear their gas masks at the German High Seas Fleet surrender. On the back of the card was the sentence:- "They would not trust the Huns even at the last". Many Devonport men joined the world's greatest sea-power. At the end of the Great War the Grand Fleet, when it was inspected by the King, consisted of 370 British ships with over 90,000 officers and men. It contained 31 British battleships and 9 battle-cruisers, 37 light cruisers, 7 aircraft carriers, 178 destroyers and 48 submarines.

Khaki on Parade

Civilians were welcome to watch the parades in the Raglan Barracks. As a boy the author remembers the parades and on Sunday mornings the pleasure of being allowed on the parade ground to join other children and adults to listen to the band. A less happy event was standing in Cumberland Gardens and seeing a military funeral with the gun carriage leaving the barracks and slowly making its way to the Garrison Church.

First Devonport Caravan

The caravan, believed to have been the first built in Devonport, was constructed in 1930 in the workshops in Mount Street. The vehicle is standing inside South Raglan Barracks, outside the officers' quarters. The small girl on the left holding a crystal ball is Mrs. Betty Elliot nee Potter. Mr. and Mrs. Frederick are also in the photograph.

Promoted to Glory

Number One Corps of the Salvation Army look smart wearing white sashes and arm bands. It is possible that they are in mourning for William Booth or his wife's funeral. The white sashes are believed to be for purity. Some of those in the group were; Nurse Polmeer, Fred Perry, Beatrice Gordon, Margaret Ward and Joe Rothery. Granby Street was very near Fore Street and Marlborough Street.

Army Ladies

The Salvation Army receives great support from such female supporters as shown in this group. The author remembers in later years the enthusiasm that existed during a march of Sunday School pupils and teachers led by the Salvation Army in 1953 to the Scott Memorial area at Mount Wise for a combined service on the green slopes. The Minister was the Reverend Ewart Lewis of the Methodist Central Hall, Fore Street.

Treat in Store

So runs the wording in the centre of the photograph. It was a treat for the people of Devonport to see the Salvation Army Band marching through the streets. Sometimes the instruments were played by sailors who were also "Salvationists". Bill Warn is on the big drum. The group would often play in the open air on the corner of Princess Street in the vicinity of Tozers shop. On Armistice Day 11th November the band would play during a service at the War Memorial in Devonport Park.

Stoke Carnival 1973

Two of the beautiful horses driven by bowler-hatted gentlemen were part of the scene in the Stoke Village Carnival of 1973. Horses were used extensively in Devonport until well after the Second World War. The author remembers how one could tell the time in the mornings by the noise of horses hoofs making their way to the Dockyard. Strong horses such as those in the photograph were regularly seen outside the Cooperative Stores in Ross Street. The stables had their entrance in the lane at the back of the store, which ran parallel with Albert Road.

Oil Tanks On Fire!

The author, when a boy sitting in the air raid shelter in Devonport Park, heard the voice of Mr. Wilkes the Air Raid Warden, shouting "The oil tanks over in Torpoint have been hit. I want volunteers to go over on the ferry to fight the fire". The oil tanks are seen behind Simmonds Brewery, in the more peaceful time of 1973. Devonport Secondary School, whose headteacher is Mr. H. W. Worrall, B.A., is situated to the right of the scene.

Redskins On The Wagon

Whether dancing around the totem pole in the Stoke Carnival of 1973 or around the stage of the bandstand in nearby Devonport Park in the 1930s, the Geraldine Lambs dancers give much pleasure to those fortunate enough to see them.

Watch This Space

The Hall now known as The Queen Victoria Masonic Hall, on the corner of Kathleaven Street, is situated half-way up on the right. Opposite the hall was eventually built the State Cinema (now the Mayflower), soon after the outbreak of war in 1939. The houses at the top of the picture in Vicarage Road later named Normandy Way, mark the route that the American troops took on their way to their invasion embarkation point in June 1944 (which was in the vicinity of the Brunel Bridge).

'Ello, 'Ello, 'Ello

The police box in Saint Budeaux Square (Wolseley Road) was an essential link for information for the policeman on the beat. When its amber light began to flash policemen in the vicinity would hasten to answer an emergency call on the phone inside. If a policeman had a prisoner he could be locked inside the box until reinforcements came. Lost children and animals have also found refuge in the police boxes. The last operational police box with its "Doctor Who" type flashing amber lamp was the 50 year old blue box in Outland Road which was opened up for every Plymouth Argyle match.

Keeping Their Chins Up

Two hours after the King and Queen left the city, having spoken to Women Air Raid Wardens and inspected sailors in the Royal Naval Barracks, the most devastating air raid yet experienced took place on March 20th 1941. The King and Queen, who had been looking at the damage done in earlier raids left with the words of an air raid warden, "We're keeping our chins up" fresh in their minds.

Hello and Goodbye

Many sailors who lived in Devonport said their hellos and goodbyes at Keyham G.W.R. Station, which was near the Royal Naval Barracks. A railway track existed in the R.N. Barracks to connect with the main line. The author remembers leaving Devonport at this station complete with kit bag to join a troopship en-route to join H.M.S. *Flamingo* in the Persian Gulf.

Stop All Traffic!

Not a single train crossed the Tamar River for two hours, when Isambard Kingdom Brunel, the creative genius of the Great Western Railway, made an inspection of the Royal Albert Bridge. He had been unable to attend the official opening of one of his greatest engineering feats. Later, although ill and dying, Brunel made the inspection tour by being towed across the bridge on a flat truck. The river at this point was 1,100 feet wide. The Admiralty needed the bridge to give 100 feet of headroom. Although not as efficient nor as quiet as modern diesels the steam trains were loved by many people.

Porter!

In the days when porters with trucks at the ready to help passengers with their heavy cases were always available, Ford South Western Station was a busy place. 1890 saw the opening of the Plymouth, Devonport and South Western Line from Lydford through Tavistock and Bere Alston to Devonport.

The Gun Wharf

Situated approximately between Cornwall Street and Pottery Quay is the Gun Wharf. (1941 it became Morice Yard and was integrated into the Dockyard). The land was acquired by the War Department in 1718. A row of houses was built inside for the Senior Officers about 1720. There were two main store houses, three storeys high, containing a powder magazine, sheds for gun carriages, vast piles of muskets, pistols, cutlasses, grapeshot and other stores.

Roll up! Roll up!

Outside the Gun Wharf wall and inside the large open space in front of the Torpoint Ferry gates was the site of a permanent Whiteleggs Fair. The author remembers the music, dodgems and bright lights that were "eliminated" with the advent of the war in 1939. In Devonport's harbour can be seen a small aircraft carrier plus a "pack" of small submarines with its parent ship. One such ship the 9,000-tonne former submarine depot ship, H.M.S. Forth, the Royal Navy's oldest warship afloat was to be scrapped in July, 1985 after seven years of lying idle in the River Tamar.

Jack and Jill

These trousered Wrens in the early days of the war wore soft floppy hats. Their attitude to their task was, however, far from floppy. They manned the harbour boats, drove trucks, repaired guns and torpedoes, and were despatch riders on motor cycles. They performed many duties, and members of the Womens Royal Naval Service were a great asset. It was a Wren Petty Officer named Vera Rich who drove King George VI when he visited Dartmouth in 1942. The two despatch outriders were also Wrens.

And then Came the Yanks

Why did a large group of American soldiers and sailors leave the Friendship Inn situated in Albert Road; cross to the bottom of Ross Street slope (near to the present site of Deveonport Secondary School) where I was standing with some other boys, and begin viciously fighting with four British sailors? The sailors were probably from H.M.S. Raleigh as they looked very young. The fighting continued until a Royal Naval Police Patrol charged down the slope scattering the Americans who ran towards Devonport Park where the U.S. Army had quarters. As one of the U.S. soldiers ran up the lane between Milne Place and Hood Street I saw one of the patrol throw his tin helmet at him catching the "escapee" on the back of the leg. The feelings of the locals ran very high over this fight. It was not until forty years later that I found the answer to the puzzling question as to why it began.

The Americans arrived in Devonport in the Spring of 1943. I remember seeing the first "snappy" jeep being driven down Milne Place with the insignia of the white star that was carried by many U.S. vehicles. Apart from such areas in Devonport Park they occupied the Raglan Barracks. Soon the Stars and Stripes "Old Glory" was flying from the old Admiralty House at Mount Wise. Hamoaze House was their naval headquarters. A familiar sight soon to be seen on Devonport street corners were these American servicemen. There were hostels in the city for white Americans and another well equipped hostel for coloured members of the United States forces. During the build up to D-Day General Dwight Eisenhower, the Supreme Allied Commander-in-Chief could be seen in a military cavalcade with armed motor cycle outriders.

For a while there was a reciprocal friendship between the Americans and locals. They had a respect for the people who had endured so much from the air raids. In return the Yanks were liked because of their happy-go-lucky and very generous nature. Many people retained this impression of the Americans. However, in Morice Town attitudes changed and many locals grew to dislike them. Living so close to the large camp of U.S. servicemen one became aware of the frequency of fights that broke out mainly among themselves. One evening soon after the Americans had occupied Devonport Park, I was talking with my friends to two American Privates at the junction of Ross Street and Hood Street. A sergeant of the U.S. army asked them if they had passes to be out of camp. We were amazed to see the two soldiers circling around the sergeant with knives at the ready. Order was restored when other troops arrived on the scene. Unruly behaviour was often checked by their service police conspicuous with white helmet, white gloves, white belt, white gaiters and heavy truncheon on display. I saw one U.S. soldier who had been quickly bundled into a jeep, near the bottom of Albert Road, change his mind about getting out again when one of these truncheons was raised above his head.

Reading a local newspaper in 1984 I read an account relating to an incident that happened in April 28th 1944. An American sailor witnessed the loss of over 700 United States servicemen during a training exercise for D-Day. A convoy of American landing craft were attacked by German high speed torpedo boats, called E-boats near Blackpool Sands, Slapton in Devon. The Americans ignored their training and opened fire without orders. They killed scores of their own men. Later, because of the mistaken belief that it was the fault of the British Navy many terrible fights took place, not only in Devonport such as the one I witnessed, but in places such as Fowey and Falmouth.

In retrospect it was not surprising that hostility arose between some of the local residents who had been under the strain of war conditions since 1939 and some of the American servicemen who had to undergo the stress of preparing for the invasion of Europe. In later years, under peace time conditions, I met many U.S. servicemen when serving with the Royal Navy in the Persian Gulf and found them to be very conscientious and likeable individuals.

Although the incident that took place near the *Friendship Inn* caused ill feeling between the locals and the U.S. servicemen, the people of Devonport knew they had much to thank the Americans for during the war. This included the help given to morale through the brilliant talents of such individuals as Fred Astaire, Shirley Temple and Bing Crosby. Their films were enjoyed by many in cinemas such as the Forum in Fore Street.

Pym Street

The green slopes of Devonport Park at the end of Pym Street hold many memories for the author. Prior to the erecting of the Public Air Raid Shelter on the right hand side of the path, the preliminary trenches made a first class "playground". British soldiers covered the area when relaxing prior to continuing their march to the railway station. Later, the American soldiers played volley ball on the flat area over the top of the shelters.

Name *Horace Ernest Meech Noyes*

Ship's Name	List and No.	Rating	From	To	Cause of Discharge
Impregnable	J.2154	Boy 2 Cl	14 Oct 24	5 Mch 25	
Ganges	15/930	—"—	6 Mch 25	30 May 25	
"	"	Boy 1 Cl WT	31 May 25	28 Nov 25	
"	"	Ord Tel	29 Nov 25	5 Jan 26	
"Hood"	5² 529	—"—	6 Jan 26	24 Mch 27	
—"—	" "	Telegraphist	25 Mch 27	29 Apl 27	
Vivid	15 2542	—"—	30 Apl 27	16 Apl 28	
"Cornwall"	5² 229	—"—	17 Apl 28	12 Feb 31	
Vivid	15 5085	—"—	13 Feb 31	23 Apl 31	
"Norfolk"	5² 318	—"—	24 Apl 31	21 Apl 32	
Vivid (Warwick)	5² 140	—"—	22 Apl 32	10 Jan 33	
Vivid	15 331	—"—	11 Jan 33	14 Feb 33	
Osprey	5ᵀ 576	—"—	15 Feb 1933	13 Oct 1933	
Vivid	15 458	—"—	14 Oct 33	31 Dec 1933	
Drake	15 458	—"—	1 Jan 34	8 Mch 34	
Calcutta	15²/150	—"—	9 Mch 34	25 May 34	
Gannet	5² 108	—"—	26 May 34	19 May 36	
Dauntless		—"—	20 May 36	30 Jul 36	
Drake		—"—	31 July 36	22 Sep 36	
Drake (Centurion)		—"—	23 Sep 36	19 Apr 37	
Colombo (Caledon)		—"—	20 Apl 37	15 Oct 37	
Drake		—"—	16 Oct 37	20 Feb 38	
Pembroke (Whitehall)		—"—	21 Feb 38	7 Apl 38	
Drake (———)		—"—	8 Apl 38	13 May 38	
Drake		—"—	14 May 38	3 June 38	
Drake (Gipsy)		—"—	4 June 38	22 July 38	
(———)		—"—	25 Jul 38	31 Aug 39	

And See The World

Horace Ernest Meech Noyes, the author's step-father joined the Royal Navy as a Boy Second Class in 1924. One of the perks of joining up, a tot of rum, was not issued until "Man's Service" was reached at eighteen. Commissions abroad would last for over two years and after a short spell of leave a further Commission perhaps in China would result. One of the famous ships upon which he served in 1927 was the battleship H.M.S. *Hood*. She was lost in 1941 with only 3 survivors. Horace was himself a survivor when H.M.S. *Gipsy*, a destroyer, was blown in two after hitting a mine in 1939. The *Illustrious* which he joined in April 1940 was severely damaged by enemy action in Malta and went to the U.S. Navy Yard at Norfolk, Virginia, U.S.A., for repairs. In the August, 1941, soon after Horace joined the *Malaya*, Lord Louis Mountbatten became the Captain of H.M.S. *Illustrious*.

Ship	Rating	From	To	
Maidstone II (Gipsy)	Tel	1 Sep 39	31 Oct 39	
Drake IV (Gipsy)	—"—	1 Nov 39	21 Nov 39	
Drake	—"—	22 Nov 39	10 Mch 40	
—"—	A/Lg. Tel.	11 Mch 40	30 Mch 40	
Victory	—"—	31 Mch 40	15 Apl 40	
Illustrious	—"—	16 Apl 40	10 Mch 41	
—"—	Lg. Tel.	11 Mch 41	9 June 41	
Malaya	—"—	10 June 41	5 Aug 41	
Drake	—"—	6 Aug 41	23 Sept 41	
Eagle	—"—	24 Sep 41	10 Apl 42	
Drake	—"—	11 Apl 42	31 May 42	
Ferret (Birage)	—"—	1 June 42	30 Sept 44	
Eaglet (—"—)	—"—	1 Oct 44	4 Apl 45	
Drake	—"—	5 Apl 45	6 Nov 45	
Boscawen (Golden Fleece)		7 Nov 45	15 Nov 45	
Lanka (—"—)		16 Nov 45	31 Dec 45	
Highflyer (—"—)	—"—	1 Jan 46	15 Aug 46	
Lochinvar (—"—)		16 Aug 46	31 Jan 47	
Tartar (Golden Fleece)		1 Feb 47	24 Apl 47	
Drake		25 Apl 47	24 November 1947	Pensioned d° 54 Released
Drake		25 Nov 47	27 Jan 48	

Horace being a wireless telegraphist spoke highly of Lord Louis who at one time was Fleet Wireless Operator. Lord Louis took pride in the fact that he knew each wireless operator by name. He also was proud of the Royal Navy's achievement during hostilities and said that the Navy had come out of World War II with great credit.

In 1931, Horace, like many other junior ratings, was ordered to take a 25% pay cut, reducing pay by 1 shilling and twopence out of four shillings (20p) a day. This brought about the mutiny at Invergordon. These drastic cuts were cancelled but the pay, that by 1931 had not been increased for 12 years, was not in fact increased until 1944 when it rose to 5 shillings a day. Horace survived the war leaving H.M.S. *Drake* at Keyham to be pensioned off in 1948.

In The Front Line
When the Germans gained control of the coast on the French side of the Channel, we were in great danger. Individual control of sirens were put under single remote control at the Greenbank police headquarters where an electric switch activated sirens at the Plymouth Guildhall tower, Milehouse, Ker Street, Camels Head, St. Budeaux and Crownhill. The family in the Anderson air raid shelter were unhurt during the first raid when a bomb fell on Swilly on Saturday 6th July 1940.

Gas!
The words in the right hand lower corner say it all. "Danger! Gas". In the heavily blitzed area of Goschen Street Keyham, near the Dockyard, an area is roped off to keep the public away. Despite this precaution two small boys who played among the ruins twenty four hours after the Mustard Gas demonstration by the decontamination squad in September 1942 developed mustard blisters and were taken to hospital.

Theory And Practice
From September, 1939, emergency measures to meet air attacks were practised. In Milne Place the author watched the volunteers of the Street Fire Party under Mr. Lee (of 1 Milne Place) running out the hoses in preparation for the worst. When it happened many bizarre things were to be seen inside the bombed houses. Despite the blast, plates stayed on walls, and some clocks continued to tick away the time.

"Bye For Now Mum"

Have you got your gas mask? This would be one of the many questions directed at the children as they were bing evacuated to safer areas. Things were fairly normal until the heavy raids of March and April, 1941. Even when the evacuation of the children took place it was voluntary. Many special trains left from North Road Station to go to Cornwall. About ninety schools in the city were destroyed or severely damaged in the air raids.

White Cap Covers Will Be Worn

Not worn, however, when the author with many other Devonport boys joined the Royal Navy in August 1944 at the very exciting time when the news bulletins brought news of Allied success in France. The blue caps were finally discarded by the navy on May 1st 1956. Prior to that they were worn until the end of April and the refreshing change to white took place on 1st May. This was reversed on the last day of September when the sombre blue caps returned on 1st October.

Time For A Tune

The Royal Navy had little time for relaxation. However, a piano in one of the blitzed streets, brought a few moments of relief. The old lady on the right, who is sitting in a comfortable armchair, may have been one of Devonport's citizens who had seen the Navy including the young officers from the Royal Naval Engineering College in Keyham, (erased in 1985) participating in fire-fighting and dangerous rescue work. Gas masks and tin hats had to be carried at all times.

Follow That Car

It would have been a harrowing ride along Fore Street after the Devonport blitz. On the corner of Marlborough Street to the left of the car stood Tozers the well known local shop. Behind the car is seen the tower of Devonport Market (still standing inside the Dockyard wall). To the right of the Market's tower is the Column and to the left is the church of St. John which had an elliptical gallery.

Cinema Corner

The Electric cinema, as it eventually became known, had a tower similar in appearance to the one of Devonport Market. Unlike the market, however, it did not have a clock. It did not materialise owing to lack of finance. The Forum cinema (site still standing) stood to its left (when facing) and the site of the Tivoli Cinema stood opposite. (near to the present site of the Fore Street Methodist Central Hall).

Put Out That Light

The postcard dated 24th October, 1939, was one of many humorous ones in a time of bleakness. The "blackout" was one of the biggest difficulties with which the police had to deal. There were four murders. One of them was a Polish petty officer whose body was found in an empty raid-damaged house in Devonport. As a boy during the blackout the author, remembers wearing a badge on his coat lapel. The badges were luminous and at night prevented people from stumbling into each other. The caption on the postcard read, "Our house is the one marked with an X."

Fire Guard Duties

Only those citizens with a valid reason could be exempted from Fire Guard Duties. Thousands of incendiary bombs dropping on the congested areas of Devonport destroyed more property than that blasted into destruction. Those involved with dealing with the conflagration showed much personal bravery in many incidents.

Schools in Keppel Place

1809 Stoke Public School founded (date approx.)
1863 Alonzo J. Rider FCS, headmaster.
1899 W. H. Crang, headmaster.
1906 School transferred to Local Authority.
1908 The Foundation Stone of Devonport Higher Elementary School laid by Alderman Littlejohn, J.P., on the site of the formerly demolished Stoke Public School. Mr. G. J. Mitchell, B.A., headmaster.
1925 Renamed: Keppel Place Central School. A. L. Strachan B.A., headmaster.
1926 Boys transferred to Sutton High School for Boys in Regent Street, Plymouth. Keppel Place School renamed Stoke Damerel Secondary School for Girls.
1932 Renamed Devonport Higher Elementary for Girls.
1935 Stoke Damerel Secondary School for Girls.
1937 Stoke Damerel High School.
1984 The school's merger with Plymouth's Sutton High Boys School meant a return to the situation that existed in 1926.

CITY OF PLYMOUTH.

FIRE GUARD HEADQUARTERS,
2, Houndiscombe Villas,
Houndiscombe Road,
PLYMOUTH.

FMc/PT/1A.   Jan 18th 1943.

Mrs Kathleen Noyes.
4 Milne Place
Stoke.

Dear Madam,

With reference to your exemption from Fire Guard Duties, will you please let us have the name and address of a Friend or Neighbour please or friend as a reference to whom we can refer to substantiate your claim.

Kindly give this matter your immediate attention.

Yours faithfully,

FIRE GUARD OFFICER.

Never Too Old

One-time Devonport lad, Harold Feabes stands in the top row, second from right with other Air Raid Wardens. Some Wardens in the city were teenagers and one was eighty years old. He was awarded the British Empire Medal for devotion to duty. Wardens were well trained to deal with anti-gas, first-aid, incendiary bombs, high-explosive bombs and had a knowledge of people living in their area. When the danger of invasion was at its height many of them were trained in the use of arms with the Home Guard.

A Tale of Two Badges

Mr. S. P. Greenwood proudly wore the badge with the initials K.C.S. when he was a pupil of Keppel Place Central School in 1922. His brother Mr. H. H. Greenwood attended the Higher Elementary School which had the badge with the initials H.E.S. This metal cap badge could be bought for a shilling (five pence) at the gent's outfitters, Prynns, which was situated near the Alhambra Theatre in Devonport. The girls of the school wore their badges in their boaters.

The "Bertie Day" Shield

The first winners of the Bertie Day Shield were Keppel Place Central School in 1925. It was presented by a local celebrity Mr. Alf Day in memory of his deceased son, a former pupil of the school when it was the Devonport Higher Elementary School.

Top Row: Mr. Dean and Mr. Algate. Teachers who trained the "Under 14" team. *Row 3:* E. Gill, C. Callard, E. Hobbs, L. Nutall, A. Kelland, R. Underhay, B. Lucas, H. Horswell, S. Greenwood. *Row 2:* C. Ham, E. Holbrook, S. Pine, Mr. A. L. Strachan Headmaster, Mr. Alf Day, S. Lidstone (Capt), A. Clarry. *Row 1:* J. Cox, A. Barrett, R. Baker.

The Raised Flag

In 1915 the noble edifice in Keppel Place was known as the 1st Sectional Hospital. The Red Cross flag is flying on one of the highest buildings in Stoke Village. The original school built on this site in 1809 was much needed as it was reported in 1812 that many hundreds of children of Plymouth Dock, later named Devonport, were living in by-courts and alleys, growing up in scenes of vice and debauchery, receiving no moral, religious or secular education.

Sticks at the Ready

A "man teacher" from Saltash attended the Higher Elementary School in 1912 to take the girls for stick drill. The fourth girl from the right is Miss Winnie Linahan. A different kind of drill was carried out during the Second World War by Royal Naval Artificer Apprentices before leaving the building to march down Albert Road and into the Dockyard to work in the factory onboard the Marshal Ney.

Upstairs, Downstairs

The flat roof of the Higher Elementary School in Keppel Place was the exclusive domain of the girl pupils. The boys had to be content with the use of the basement for recreation. Girls are dancing in drill costume in 1914, when the Headmistress was Mrs. Tierney. Each year a May Queen was chosen. Teachers remembered are Miss Synor of 1A, Miss Blaze 2A, Miss Beck 3A, Miss Pearce taught Geography and Miss Wavish who travelled from Torpoint.

The Bluejackets Band

The Royal Naval Band was composed of volunteers. When they were not playing as musicians ashore they had their own jobs on H.M. ships around the world. They continued their jobs as musicians when they were not sailing. Because of this rôle the band was one of the biggest, numerically, in the world. In 1932 Leading Seaman Bush, the bandmaster, short-circuited all the trams at St. Levan Road, when his silver mace hit the overhead wires. Mr. S. Warwick of Stuart Road and Mr. Malcolm Richards were two of the members of the band that route-marched from the R.N. Barracks to Camel's Head, and then to the Naval camp at Vicarage Road in St. Budeaux.

Empire Day

The future defenders of the British Empire stand smartly to attention in the grounds of Saint James the Great School. The school was adjacent to the Church of the same name which was situated on the corner of what is now known as St. Lo's Place. In the first row second from the right stands Harry Bonning. The author remembers proudly carrying a large Union flag to Morice Town Infants School on Empire Day in the 1930's. A part of the day's proceedings would be to listen to the names of all the countries under British rule.

Putty Philpott

King of carnivals, ex-doorman of the Palace Theatre, landlord of the *No Place Inn* and sailor, were some of the jobs undertaken by this very popular citizen. Known as the Royal Navy's greatest comedian, perhaps even he would have failed to raise a smile when the Royal Navy broke with tradition by discontinuing the rum issue in 1970. The tots of rum which were abolished when Devonport's own M.P., Dr. David Owen, was Navy Minister, were first introduced into the Royal Navy in 1655 because wine and beer went sour in the barrels.

F. "PUTTY" PHILPOTT
LATE R.N. THE NAVY'S GREATEST COMEDIAN.
BRUNSWICK HOTEL
SOUTH OF THE BRICKFIELDS
Down STONEHOUSE BRIDGE Way.

Arthur L. Clamp – the man behind the books

Arthur Leslie Clamp was a man of boundless energy with a passion for helping others, particularly through his love of history. A printer by trade, he started his career in a printing company before moving his family from Exeter to Plymouth to teach at the Plymouth College of Art and Design, where he eventually became the Head of the Printing Department.

Arthur with his five children.

A Devoted Family Man

Despite his love of teaching, Arthur prioritised his family, always making it home by 5:30pm for tea. He and his wife, Rosemary, raised five children: Susan, Angela, Elizabeth, David, and Steven. Arthur would often combine his love of family and history by taking his children on Sunday walks, encouraging them to appreciate historical monuments by taking photos or making crayon rubbings of gravestones for his books. The family home at 203 Elburton Road was a hub of activity, with a large garden, featuring a two-storey fort and a makeshift swimming pool.

A Lifelong Learner and Adventurer

Arthur's thirst for knowledge extended beyond history to a deep curiosity about the world. He was passionate about exploring different cultures, traditions, and cuisines, often taking advantage of his long summer holidays as a teacher to travel to places like India, Russia, South America, the middle east and the USA, sometimes bringing one of his children along. This adventurous spirit even influenced his home life, as seen by the short-lived family tradition of steam-cooking vegetables after a trip to Iceland.

History is a prominent feature of family days out

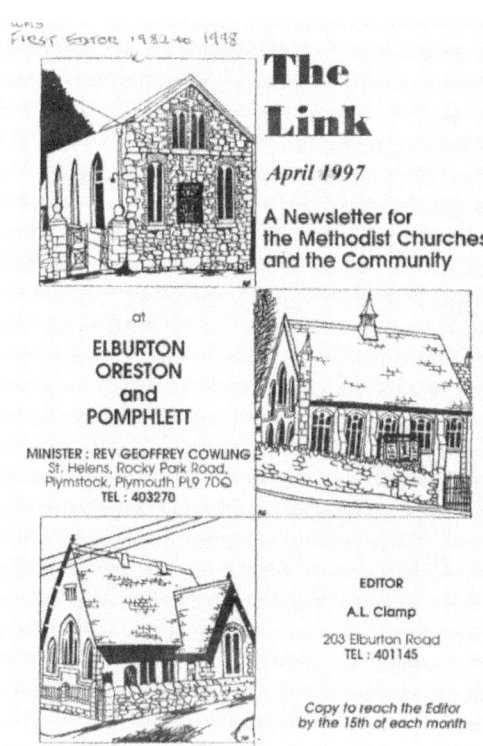

Community and Philanthropic Spirit

His commitment to serving others was evident in his long-standing involvement with the Elburton Methodist Church. He was the Sunday School Superintendent for over 15 years and served as the editor of the wider church's monthly newsletter, "The Link," for a similar duration. After Rosemary's very sad passing, Arthur later remarried and, following a chance encounter with a professor from India, established a connection with a missionary school in Chennai. Together with his new wife, Christine, he co-founded a "Sponsor a Child's Education" program that continues to this day.

*Pictured left – The cover of 'The Link' complete
with hand drawn sketches of each church by Angela
Below right – Arthur Clamp promoting his latest book
Below left – Arthur at home with his first wife, Rosemary
Below centre – Arthur on holiday with his second wife,
Christine*

A Legacy of Learning and Positivity

Arthur's greatest passion was history, which he brought to life through tireless research, documentation, and the many books he authored. He was driven by a need to "never be stuck in a rut," constantly seeking new experiences, meeting new people, and expanding his knowledge. With a positive attitude and a great sense of humour, he was always ready to help others, leaving a lasting impact on his family and community. His children, Susan, Angela, Elizabeth, David, and Steven, remember him with love and gratitude.

David Clamp, 2025

A Legacy of Local History

Below is the story of how Arthur L Clamp began writing books, in his own words, drafted shortly before he passed away in 2001. I have only made minor alterations to this text, correcting grammatical errors that he did not survive to correct himself. When I first discovered this text, I was shocked to see my name mentioned. It seems that, unbeknownst to me, I shared my first PC with him. I suspect he used it during the day when I was at school, although I do have one memory of sitting with him and showing him how it worked. It has been a pleasure to pick up where he left off and see his books republished and redistributed, and to know that I was part of the story, even back then. It was also fascinating to discover that his pricing structure matches the way I have tried to price the books, with a third going to local sellers and the rest covering printing costs with a little left over for my expenses.

I am his eldest grandson, and it is a privilege to curate his legacy, which we are calling 'The Clamp Collection'. The very last line of the text originally reads "The following pages list all the titles." Sadly, that page is missing and we have no record of all the books he published and knowing that some of those were researched by other authors makes the process of finding them even harder. I look forward to one day completing the collection and seeing them all available again. And maybe, one day, I'll even start writing my own to add to the series. For now, here is his story in his own words.

Steven Gibson, 2025

Writing and Publishing Booklets on Local Topics and Areas

I started this interest in either 1968 or 1969 when living in Woodford. I had by these dates established the Department of Printing and I think I must have been looking for something different to do. The first titles were of A5 size proofed from type set at Clarke, Doble and Brendon, Ltd., Plymouth printers, and then made up into pages and printed at Sawtell and Neilson, Ltd., Totnes.

Then began a slow process of getting them out to shops, etc. which proved to be more time consuming and difficult than actually researching, writing and getting the books into print. However, I persisted and opened a business account with Barclays Bank on the Broadway. I was advised to give it a title so I called it "Westway Publications". There came along another problem, one of storage of paper and finished books which was solved when the family moved to Elburton in 1970.

I changed the printer to Penwell, Ltd., Callington, Cornwall, as he was then just setting up himself and his prices seemed very reasonable. I did not get any of the printers to make up the complete books. I hand folded the flat printed sheets, stitched the books on a small manual table stitcher and trimmed them in a small hand turned guillotine which I bought from someone in Penzance for £40. It was brought up in a van.

The trouble and time going to and fro to Callington was too much so I transferred the printing to PDS Printers, Prince Rock, Plymouth, and I have been with them ever since. Now they are at Plympton which is easy to reach and they fold the flat sheets which was turning out to be a long chore which only saved a small part of the printing costs.

All my first titles were written by myself. I took the photographs and developed them in the loft of the house, the type was set by now on a computer situated in the house at Elburton from which I had collected photographic lengths of text to cut up and law down as pages.

At some point I decided that I would do my own film processing of lith film so I bought a large second hand process camera from Kingsbridge and learnt through trial and error to make line negatives of the text and halftone negatives of the illustrations which proved more difficult than I anticipated. The main problem was trying to keep the developer in the large dish at the correct temperature as any change would affect the developing time. I replaced this old camera with a brand new one bought from Croydon, Surrey, costing £900. This has turned out to be a great asset cutting out an expensive part of the printer's costs and one crucial aspect of the work which I could control.

By the middle 1970s there were many outlets I had contacted in Plymouth, up to Dartmoor, Exeter, around to Torbay, Totnes, Dartmouth and the South Hams. The market for local books was much greater than I had first thought and through getting to know many local people undertaking research themselves had the chance to help and make up books for other people who had in most instances, got together a collection of photographs with some text in a rather muddled way. Through my experience in print I was able to shape up their work and get it into print and in every case I had to pay the printer and let the person have the royalties. In the majority of titles produced in this manner this was another way of producing titles and it did give some profit to my work. However, I must say that in a few cases I lost out by either the other person getting the numbers wrong, not returning any monies from stock I delivered or they thought that more of their books should have been sold.

The print run was usually 1,000 copies and from time to time I have had reprints of 250 copies. It took about ten years to clear the first print run so I always had large stocks in the garage, workshop, etc. The numbers sold during the early years was about 7,000 copies a year increasing to around 9,000 copies and for the whole of the enterprise about 500,000 have been sold. The booklets have become part of the local scene and many people collect them, shops regularly order copies and I go around certain areas month by month restocking or replacing titles as necessary.

During the past year or so I have started setting the text on a Packard Bell PC, something which I should have done some years back. I share it with Steven Gibson, my grandson. There appears to be no end to the market for local books, but I could not earn a regular income because of the long time it takes to sell stock.

However, now exceeding 100 titles made up mainly of A4 twenty-four page booklets, some folded guides, with selling prices set with a third going to the shop which is the trade custom, the original idea has been quite successful and could go on for ever.

Apart from monetary benefits, however spasmodically these might be, I have learnt a lot myself, met many interesting people and have become part of the local scene with requests to give talks and to advise people about getting into print.

Arthur L Clamp, 2001

This newspaper article, published by the Evening Herald on 17th August 2001, forms a good record of his life. Just as he encourages us to learn more about local history, we encourage you to learn a little about him. For that reason, we have included these pages at the back of all the most recently republished books, in honour of his memory and recognition of his contribution to the community.

www.ingramcontent.com/pod-product-compliance
Lightning Source LLC
Chambersburg PA
CBHW061407070526
44584CB00031B/4181